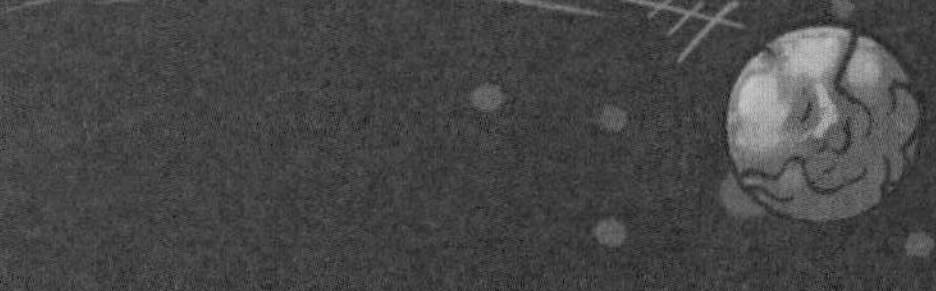

THE POO-NIVERSE

By Paul Mason and Fran Bueno

WAYLAND

www.waylandbooks.co.uk

First published in Great Britain in 2021 by Wayland

Text and illustrations copyright © Hodder & Stoughton, 2021

Editors: Elise Short and Grace Glendinning
Designer: Peter Scoulding
Illustrations: Fran Bueno

ISBN: 978 1 5263 1439 0 HBK

ISBN: 978 1 5263 1441 3 PBK

An imprint of
Hachette Children's Group
Part of Hodder & Stoughton

Carmelite House
50 Victoria Embankment
London EC4Y 0DZ

An Hachette UK Company
www.hachette.co.uk
www.hachettechildrens.co.uk

Printed in Dubai

Picture credits:
Alamy: Album 22, 26t, 28; Blue Planet Archive 41; GL Archive 34; Grant Heliman 18; NASA 33; Vintage Space 12; Water Frame 10.

Getty Images; Adrian Dennis 5.

NASA: 4, 8.

PA Archive/PA Images/Ben Birchall: 15t.

Shutterstock: Altrendo Images 39b; andregric 17 c; Gratsias Adhi Hermawan 29, Nikolay Antonov 13tl; AP 30;

Begun1983 14bl; Peppo Chadisorn 25cr; Thatsanaphong Chanwarin 15b; Alex Coan 35;

Mandy Creighton 7 b; Crevis cover, 37; CV Stock 25t; Oleg D 21t; Nagy Dodo 17 t; Elster 6c; Emka7 4 4tr; Everett Collection 39t; David Gallagher 7 t; Gengis 90 20b; Guy42 4cr; Thanakorn Hongphan 6t; Horus2017 4tl; Vadim Hunko 43; Inspire finder 14br; Eric Isselee 11; Andrea Izzotti 41; Kacutta 43;Alexey Khromusin 24; Sergiy Kuzmin 25cl; Natalia Maksymenko 17 t; Nixx Photography 20t; Photochur 26b; Pingdao and NASA 8b; Prostock studio 29; Dwi Putra stock 20c; Milton Rodriguez 22-23; Santana 4cl;

Shchus 17 b; Cass Tippit 13tr; Mr Prawet Thadthiam 21b; Peter Vanco 8-9.

CONTENTS

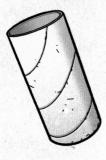

From the smallest to the largest, human to animal, the runniest to the hardest, the top stinkers to the sweet-smellers, the floatiest to the sinkiest, this book is full of facts about poo. Prepare to be swept away by an information poo-nami!

Poo-fume

Ask people to say one word describing poo, and the chances are they will say 'smelly', 'stinky' or something similar. They would be wrong – at least in parts of the animal world. Otters (whose poos are called spraints), elephants and koalas (whose poos smell of minty-fresh eucalyptus*) are among the animals whose poos smell quite nice.

Even human poo contains a chemical called skatole that is used in many perfumes. Of course there's also all those OTHER smells in our poo ...

*It's a good job koala poo smells OK, as they produce about 360 poos a day and even poo while they're asleep.

Whenever I see it, I plant my knees in the grass, lean over and draw its delicious smell into my lungs.
– a wildlife photographer describes spotting a piece of otter poo

Early explorers of the poo-niverse faced great challenges. Find out more on pages 32–33.

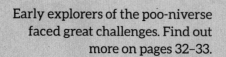

Happy pooing

Most people agree that it is very satisfying to have a really good poo. But why is this?

Doing a big poo stimulates something called the vagus nerve. It causes your heart rate and blood pressure to drop. Then extra blood starts flowing to your brain. Usually this produces that familiar feeling of happiness ... but in extreme cases, it causes people to pass out.

WORLD'S SMELLIEST JOBS: SEWER CLEANER

Sewers are underground passageways that carry away our poo. They need to be cleaned regularly to stop them becoming blocked.

Sewers don't usually get blocked by poo alone. First, wet wipes and other items get snagged and start to build up. Then, cooking fat that people have poured down the drain starts to build up on the wipes. Soon a 'fatberg' has grown. One of the world's biggest fatbergs was discovered in a sewer in Liverpool, UK in 2019. It was bigger than a jumbo jet.

CERTAINLY DOESN'T SMELL OF FRIED FOOD ANY MORE ...

Golden poo

Would we be so fast to flush if we knew our poo contained gold? Well, yes, we should probably keep flushing – a single person's poo only contains the tiniest bit – definitely not enough to make it worth sorting through the mess at home. (See page 13 for details on where the gold comes from and how much it's worth.)

Some animal poo is much more valuable than ours. Sperm whales' poo (or sometimes vomit) contains a substance called ambergris, which is used in perfume. Just a few grammes of this precious poo is worth hundreds of pounds.

Poo is basically food. Not food you'd want to eat, of course – although some animals DO like to snack on their own poo, or even their mum's. This has never really caught on among humans.

Poo is food with most of the useful stuff sucked out of it by the digestive system. In mammals, the process works in a similar way whether you are a human or a hedgehog, kangaroo or capybara.

When you eat something, it gets chewed, then swallowed down to your stomach. (As long as you have one: see **Four stomachs, and none** on page 7.)

Digestive process:

1 minute after entering body
The food arrives in the stomach. It is churned around and becomes a liquid called chyme.

2–6 hours later
The chyme enters the small intestine, where almost all of the nutrients are sucked out of it and into the blood.

3–5 hours later
The chyme – which is now much more sludgy – enters the large intestine. Here, bacteria break down the last useful bits. As part of the process, they produce gas.

Most of the water has now been sucked out of the chyme. It passes slowly through the last bit of the large intestine.

24–48 hours later
What's left at the end emerges as poo.

mother's milk poo

Lots of baby animals eat their mum's poo. They include elephants, hippos and koalas.

This sounds revolting to a human, but there is a good reason for it. The poo contains bacteria that help the animal digest food. Eating it gives the babies the best possible chance of surviving.

YUM!

FOUR STOMACHS, AND NONE

Animals such as cows and deer eat food that takes a long time to digest. Their stomachs are divided into four separate chambers, each with its own digestive job.

Other animals manage OK with no stomach at all. These include the duck-billed platypus and about a quarter of all fish.

THAT'S NOT MY STOMACH RUMBLING ...

Poo piles

Not all poos come out the same shape. Wombat poo, for example, is shaped a bit like a little loaf of bread. These cubes of poo are used to mark territory, like many poos in the wild, but see page 40 for more of the science behind the creation of these poo-cubes.

What does YOUR poo actually contain? Poo is a rich mixture of things your body is getting rid of.

water + mucus = comfort

The biggest single element in a human poo is water. For comfortable visits to the toilet, water needs to make up about 33 per cent of a poo*. The water makes the poo slippery and soft enough to pass through your body. As it moves along, poo also gets coated in a slimy substance called mucus, for an even smoother ride.

*See pages 44–45 for what happens when poo is too hard or too sloppy.

Bacteria, dead and alive

About 25 per cent of poo is made up of dead bacteria and another 25 per cent is made up of living bacteria. Bacteria are very, very small, so you can fit a LOT of them into a quarter of a poo.

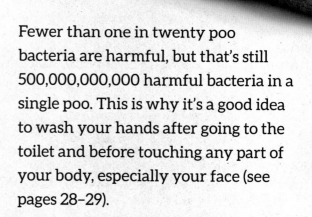

An average-size poo contains 10,000,000,000,000 bacteria.

The whole world contains 7,770,354,000 people (estimated, March 2020).

Fewer than one in twenty poo bacteria are harmful, but that's still 500,000,000,000 harmful bacteria in a single poo. This is why it's a good idea to wash your hands after going to the toilet and before touching any part of your body, especially your face (see pages 28–29).

WHAT MAKES POO BROWN?

Poo is brown because it contains bits of old blood cells. These have had a long journey through your body before they end up in poo. (Bits of old blood cells are also what cause your wee to be a yellowish colour.)

Human poo isn't always brown. It sometimes comes out red, maroon, black, pinkish, pale yellow or green. This is often a sign that the poo-er is unwell and should visit a doctor.

The other bits

About 7 per cent of a human poo is made up of things that do not break down inside your body, such as salt. Roughly 6 per cent is fibre from food. Poo also contains small amounts of fungi, viruses and other tiny organisms. There are also tiny 'microplastics', which come from food and drinks packaging, from eating food such as fish, and even from the air we

POO BRAIN

Scientists showed years ago that your intestines – where poo is made – can work without your brain. They did this using a guinea pig colon that had been removed from the guinea pig. Placing a pellet at one end caused the colon to start working, contracting and expanding to process it all the way to the end.

Flies are attracted to poo because, to them, it's both food (gross!) and a place to lay eggs. Flies lay eggs in poo because it provides a built-in feast for hatched larvae. (See page 17.)

THE WORLD'S BIGGEST POOS

Not all poos are equal. Some animals produce a huge amount of poo. The animal that is likely to have produced the most poo ever, though, might come as a surprise.

POO SIZE

Poos tend to be bigger if you eat a lot of fibre and drink a lot of water. You'll understand why if you imagine a bowlful of porridge oats that have soaked overnight in lots of water. The fibre in your poo puffs up in the same way as the oats.

Big animal = big poo

An animal's size affects how big its poo is. Big animals need a lot of energy, so they have to eat a lot. The more an animal eats, the more it is likely to poo. This means the world's biggest poos probably belong to the world's biggest animals – blue whales. Of course, there are some problems with weighing a blue whale's poo.

Weighing a blue whale's poo is a tricky job. But a mammal that eats up to 3.6 tonnes of food a day MUST have a large output.

On land, African elephants are the biggest living animal. Their poo is easier to weigh than a whale's, of course, so we know that just one elephant can produce up to 135 kg of poo a day. That's roughly the same as two grown-ups weigh.

Of course, even bigger animals once stalked the Earth. Giant dinosaurs such as *Diplodocus* seem to have had similar digestive systems to cows ... but they weighed a whole lot more (see page 35).

Cow weight: 500–750 kg
Daily cowpat output: 25–60 kg

Large sauropod weight: 50 tonnes
Daily sauropod-pat output: unknown, but a lot

History's biggest poo-ers?

By 2020, all the humans that had ever lived were estimated to have produced just over 2 billion tonnes of poo. Because there are so many of us, humankind will eventually out-poo every other animal – if we haven't already.

If all that human poo could be turned into a massive, continuous log, it would stretch over 130 billion km. Put another way, humans' historical poo would reach to the Sun and back five times.

Humans have produced a LOT of poo through history. Some of it only finally rotted away and disappeared after being put to work in surprisingly useful ways.

Growing food

You might be surprised to hear that quite a lot of our food is grown using human poo. It is treated to make it safe, renamed 'biosolid' and spread on fields to help fertilise crops. Human poo has been used as fertiliser for centuries. Hundreds of years ago in Japan, the poo of the ruling samurai was worth twice as much as a poor person's poo. The samurai got better food, so their poo contained more nutrients that would help plants grow.

WORLD'S SMELLIEST JOBS: NIGHT-SOIL MAN

Working all night when you should be asleep makes a job difficult enough. But imagine if your night-time job was collecting other people's jobbies.

Before the invention of sewers and flushing toilets, that was just what 'night-soil men' did in European cities. All night they collected poo from people's homes. The men shovelled the poo into wicker baskets and took it away to be sold as fertiliser.

LET US IN!

worm bog

Using human poo as fertiliser has health risks because the poo may contain viruses and harmful bacteria. Today, worm toilets can help treat human waste quickly (and reduce the overall poo-pile enormously). Inside, a team of worms chews through and cleans up the poo.

Panning for gold in poo

We learned on page 5 that each of our poos contain a minuscule amount of gold. It also includes other precious metals, including platinum, silver and titanium. These get into our bodies in a variety of ways, including through beauty and cleaning products, and from clothing. If you could covmpile enough poo, all those minuscule amounts would add up. In 2017 it was estimated that a million Americans produced poo containing 13 million dollars' worth of precious metal every year. Now all someone needs to do is find a way of getting hold of it.

Other surprising uses for poo

Human poo has a lot of surprising possible uses. Not every one of these has been put into practice, but experts have shown they are possible:

- making bricks for homebuilding
- making fuel briquettes that can be burned instead of wood
- squeezing out water for treating, then drinking (see page 31)
- as animal feed
- creating hydrogen fuel.

HYDROGEN FUEL RESEARCH CENTRE

The human body is very good at removing the energy from poo. Good, but not perfect – because there's still some energy left in your poo when it leaves you.

ONLY 5% CHARGE LEFT! I WONDER …

Power from poo

An average piece of poo contains a similar amount of energy to a banana – roughly 100 calories. Since most deliveries of poo contain two pieces, each visit to the toilet produces about 200 calories. In theory, this is enough energy to charge your phone 20 times or more.

Charging your phone using the energy contained in poo = not really something you can do at home.

Some of the energy is lost while poo is being turned into a form we can use, such as methane or carbon dioxide. Even so, the world's poo could provide a lot of energy – according to some estimates:

- 💩 in total people release roughly 10,000 terajoules of energy through their bottoms every day

- 💩 our daily poo energy could be converted to power for 138 million homes.

GRUESOME POO-SOME: DANGER GAS

In the time of the night-soil men you read about on page 12, many homes had cesspits where their sewage was stored until it could be taken away. The removal work had to happen at night because the smells released from the pits were SO revolting. These cesspits also sometimes released toxic gas – and occasionally even blew up.

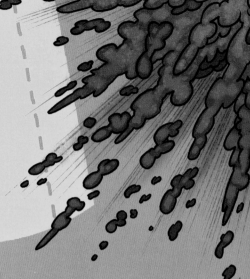

The Number 2 bus

Cars and buses don't only run on petrol, diesel or electricity – they can also run on poo gas. In Norway, the city of Oslo converted a fleet of 80 buses to run on poo gas in 2009. And in Bristol, UK, the Biobus was launched in 2015. It could travel 300 km on a tankful of poo gas, and ran along the Number 2 route.

An anaerobic digestor in use.

GAS EMISSIONS

Gas from poo can be used to provide us with power. The power can be created in two ways.

1 Boiling sewage sludge at high pressure, then quickly releasing the pressure. This makes the sludge safer and more biodegradable. It can also be used to produce fertiliser from sewage.

2 Sealing the sludge in an airless container, where it is consumed by micro-organisms. They produce gas as they eat, which can be removed and used. This process is called anaerobic digestion.

POO SNACKS

GNNNAAARGH!

IT'S NOT LIKE THERE ARE DOGS' TOILETS ANYWHERE ...

If you've ever accidentally stepped in a dog poo, you probably think there's only one thing to do with left-behind animal poo: pick it up and throw it away. But you'd be wrong.

A surprising number of animals use other animals' left-behind poo as a food source. (Yes, we did say 'food source'.)

Eating other animals' poo

You now know that there are small amounts of nutrition in poo, and some animals are determined to get at the left-behind goodness. Elephant poo, for example, is popular with animals from baboons to honey badgers and meerkats. Some are hunting for undigested food that's been pooed out. Others pick through the poo looking for the bugs and insects that make their home in elephant dung.

YUM, GRUBS!

Insect dinners

Many insects love other animals' poo. Some lay their eggs in it so that when the eggs hatch there will be something for the larvae to eat straight away. Other insects eat the poo themselves. Dung beetles, for example, have special adaptations for poo-eating. Young dung beetles can only eat solids, but adult dung beetles grow a special mouthpart that allows them to suck up liquid poo, too.

HEY, LEAVE ME SOME LIQUID!

YOU'RE NOT OLD ENOUGH YET.

Delicious dinners can cause arguments about who got the best helping.

Eating their own poo

Eating your own poo would be a BIT less revolting than eating someone else's – but not much. Even so, rabbits, hares, chimpanzees and dogs are among the animals that think nothing of snacking on their own poo. Guinea pigs can even DIE if they don't get to eat their own poo.

DO I SMELL DINNER?

Rats (and mice) sometimes nibble other animals' poo to find bits of undigested food.

GOTTA HAVE THAT POO!

POO MEDICINE

Animals sometimes eat poo because they are not feeling well. (Imagine if we started using this as medicine for kids. It would definitely cut down on school sick days.) Dogs, for example, may eat their own poo because there is something missing from their diet or something wrong with their digestion. They may be trying to reprogramme their digestive system.

Rabbits and hares eat their own poo every day. When it is pooed out the first time, they eat it straight down again while it's warm. The poo goes through their digestive system a second time, to make sure all the nutrients have been removed. When it is pooed out for a second time, the poo is left behind.

WEAPONISED POO

To most of us, poo is not very pleasant stuff, and we'd rather avoid it if we can – so it's no wonder that some animals use their poo as a way to discourage unwelcome attention.

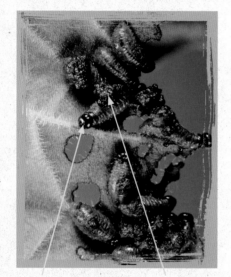

Larva   Poisonous poo

Poisonous poo

The larvae of three-lined potato beetles eat nightshade plants (among other things). These plants are poisonous. Fortunately for the beetle, though, the poison passes right through them and exits in their poo. Poisonous poo is too good to waste, so the larvae smear it on to their own backs. It becomes an excellent defence against anything that might otherwise eat the larvae before they mature.

Poo defences

Some animals use left-behind poo as camouflage or a disguise. Predators sometimes hide their natural smell by rolling in strong-smelling poo (or wee). This makes it easier for them to creep up on their prey. This is probably why pet dogs love to roll in stinky-smelling stuff: they are copying the actions of their wolf ancestors.

I CAN SMELL YOU.

WHY POO SMELLS

Poo smells because of bacteria. As they digest food, bacteria produce chemicals that smell when released into the outside world. Some of the key offenders in human poo are:

- skatole, possibly the stinkiest of all
- indole, which comes from digesting broccoli, Brussels sprouts, turnips, cabbage and other vegetables
- methyl sulphides, which are also produced by digesting cabbage and similar vegetables
- hydrogen sulphide, which has no colour unless it is burned, is corrosive, poisonous and flammable, and smells of rotten eggs.

Skatole is the worst-smelling ingredient in mammal poo. Weirdly, it actually smells nice in tiny amounts, which is why it pops up in some surprising places.

CONTAINS SKATOLE

Mammal poo

Perfume

Arum lily

Strawberry ice cream

Poo flingers

If some animals think you are getting too close, they fling poo to make you go away. If a gorilla wants to warn you off, for example, first of all it roars. Then it drums its chest. Then it throws poo at you. If none of that works, it starts pulling off bits of your body.

Hoopoe chicks also use poo to defend themselves. If you get too close they start hissing. This is rapidly followed by a powerful jet of poo, squirted at your eyes. Maybe they should be called poo-poe chicks.

Hippos also use poo to put off unwelcome visitors. They combine a wet poo, a massive fart and a whirring tail. Anything standing within about 5 m is guaranteed to get splattered.

THINGS WE DO WITH ANIMAL POO

Animals are not the only ones that find left-behind poo worthwhile. Humans have found all kinds of uses for it as well.

Add flavour to your coffee

For many years, some of the world's most-expensive coffee has been given its flavour by civets. Civets are small, fox-like animals. When it is fed coffee berries, the flesh is digested and the coffee beans pass through the civet. They emerge in its poo and, after being cleaned up, the beans are used to make coffee that tastes like no other.

Add flavour to your cheese

Poo coffee sounds pretty revolting, but probably not as revolting as maggot-poo cheese. Even so, on the Mediterranean island of Sardinia, people flavour their cheese with maggot excrement.

1 They take some innocent cheese and make a hole in the crust.

2 Cheese flies lay eggs inside, which hatch out into maggots.

3 The maggots chew their way around the cheese, digest it, then release soft, white ... well, it's basically cheesy poo.

4 The cheese is cut into thin slices and served on flatbread. If you don't want annoyed maggots to jump up as you try to eat them, you cover the flatbread with your hand.

Traditionally, Sardinians said that maggot cheese was unsafe to eat if all the maggots were dead. Either way, it is illegal to sell the cheese in many parts of the world.

20

Burn it

Dried animal poo is a popular fuel in many parts of the world. Many people burn cow dung as fuel in South Asia, Central Asia and throughout Africa. Cow-poo fuel was also used in the past in Europe and North America.

WHAT DO I DO? STUFF IT UP MY NOSTRILS?

SEVEN USES FOR ELEPHANT POO ... POSSIBLY

Around the world, people have made some pretty big claims about things elephant poo can do:

1 flavouring coffee (in the same way as civet poo)

2 repelling mosquitoes (when burnt)

3 being wrung out to provide water in an emergency

4, 5, 6 & 7 allegedly: curing headaches, unblocking sinuses, easing toothache and stopping nosebleeds*.

*We could not find proof that any of these are true.

NOW, IT NEEDS TO STEEP IN JUST-BOILED WATER FOR AT LEAST THREE MINUTES AND NOT A MOMENT LESS.

Caterpillar poo ... TEA?

In Asia, caterpillars are sometimes fed dried tea leaves. Their tiny poos are collected, added to boiling water and used to make tea. It apparently tastes quite nice!

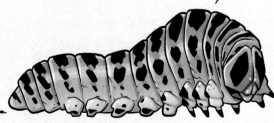

THE GUANO WAR

The Guano* War of 1864–66** is possibly the only war ever to be fought over poo. Incredibly, the war lasted over two years and involved five countries.

The Great Heap

This war was about, literally, a pile of poo. But what a pile! It was an enormous mound of bird poo known as the Great Heap. The Great Heap was 50 m tall and covered quite a lot of North Chincha Island, in the Pacific Ocean off the coast of Peru. It was extremely valuable because, at the time, guano was used to make fertiliser and gunpowder. The Great Heap was where the world's best guano was found.

Guano was mined using pickaxes. The mining was done mostly by South American prisoners and slaves, native Hawaiians and Chinese workers.

*Guano is dried bird (and bat) poo.
**The war is also known as the Chincha Islands War and the Spanish–South American War.

WHAT A HEAP OF TROUBLE!

Round 1:   Spain v. Peru

The Guano War started when Spanish troops landed on the Chincha Islands. This was a big deal: the guano there was so valuable, it produced half the Peruvian government's money each year. Spain also blockaded Peru's ports.

WHY WAS CHINCHA GUANO SO VALUABLE?

Because of their diet, seabirds' guano contains a lot of chemicals called nitrates. To grow, plants need soil that contains nitrates. If a lot of plants are grown in the same soil, though, the nitrates get used up. Spreading seabird guano on the soil adds nitrates and makes it fertile once again.

The Chincha Islands are in the perfect place to produce top-quality guano. There are millions of seabirds: boobies, pelicans, cormorants and others. Most importantly, there is little rain to wash away the nitrates in the guano.

Round 2: Spain v. Chile and Peru

In 1865, Peru's neighbour, Chile, began to support Peru. The Spanish tried to make them stop, but instead Chile declared war on Spain. Peru quickly did the same.

Round 3: Spain v. Chile, Peru, Ecuador and Bolivia

In late 1866, Ecuador and Bolivia joined the fight against Spain. A few months later the Spanish had to admit defeat.

By 1867 the Guano War was over and Peru reclaimed the Great Heap.

TOILETS THROUGH TIME

The first 'toilets' were probably just convenient trees, bushes or rivers. Ever since then, though, people have been coming up with new, better ways to get rid of their poo.

The oldest toilets

The earliest evidence of purpose-built toilets comes from either 5,000 years ago in Scotland or 3,700 years ago in Greece. (Experts are not 100 per cent certain that the Scottish toilets are really toilets.)

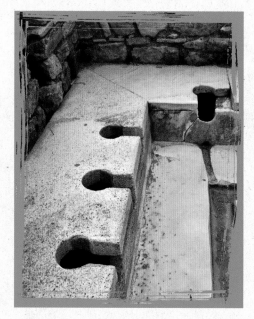

By the time of the Romans, public toilets like the one above were common: in 315 CE, Rome had 144 of them. They were communal, with holes in stone or wooden benches, where you sat and pooed while chatting to your friends.

In castles, toilets were often holes in the floor over the moat. Raiders must have had to think twice before deciding to swim across.

Washed away

If you want to get rid of a nasty, smelly poo, one of the best ways is to let nature just wash it away. On board old sailing ships, the crew used to simply poo over the side: the evidence soon disappeared astern. Toilets beside rivers offered a similar removal service, which must have been unpleasant if you were washing clothes or collecting drinking water downstream.

Flushing toilets

Flushing toilets that washed your waste away were first invented in 1592, but they didn't catch on. Most people agree that modern toilets were improved and popularised in England by a man called Thomas Crapper, in the 1860s. His machines worked alongside more modern sewers, which were needed to carry away the wastewater. Many of Crapper's designs are still being used today.

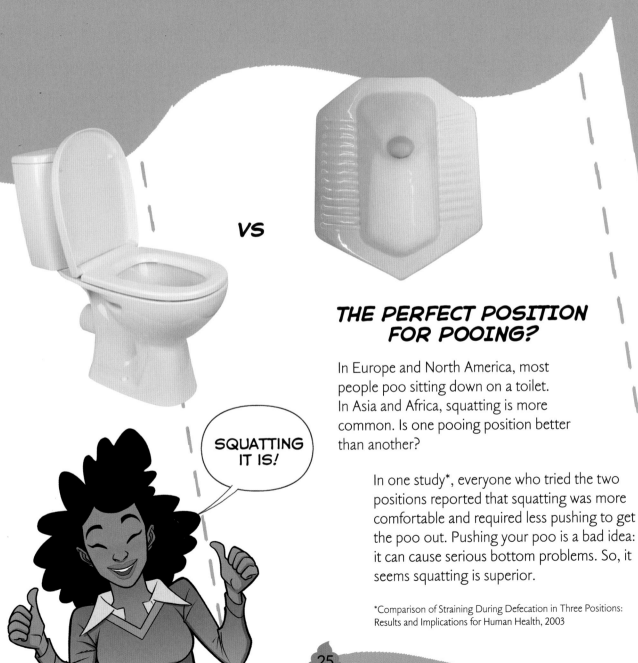

VS

THE PERFECT POSITION FOR POOING?

In Europe and North America, most people poo sitting down on a toilet. In Asia and Africa, squatting is more common. Is one pooing position better than another?

In one study*, everyone who tried the two positions reported that squatting was more comfortable and required less pushing to get the poo out. Pushing your poo is a bad idea: it can cause serious bottom problems. So, it seems squatting is superior.

*Comparison of Straining During Defecation in Three Positions: Results and Implications for Human Health, 2003

SQUATTING IT IS!

CLEANING UP

Sometimes, a poo leaves a little (or maybe a large) bit of evidence of its passing. Through history, people have used a variety of techniques for cleaning up their own personal crime scene.

PEW! CHARLIE NEEDS TO SORT THAT OUT.

YUCK! MY EYES ARE WATERING ...

first wipers

Did the first humans wipe their bottoms, about 150,000 years ago? We can't know for sure, but almost certainly not.

Humans only learned how to speak about 50,000 years ago. Before that it would have been hard to tell people delicately that a clean-up was needed.

The earliest wipers probably started cleaning themselves up using whatever was at hand: grass, soil, sand, snow or leaves, for example. As civilisation went on, though, people soon began to invent other ways to do the job.

In ancient Greece, people used pessoi: small, rounded pieces of pottery to wipe. (Or should that be poo-tery?)

Wiping sticks

In ancient Asia, it is thought Buddhist monks came up with the idea to use a wiping stick – like a very thin ruler wrapped with cloth on one end. These spread with Buddhism from south Asia to China and Japan. Wiping sticks have been found at the end of the Silk Road, dating from over 2,000 years ago.

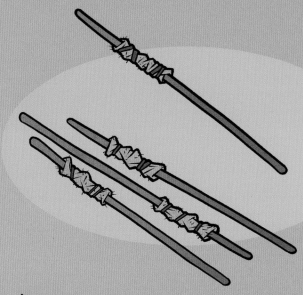

Early wipers

Roman citizens visiting the public toilets used a wet sponge on a stick. (This may have given us the expression 'getting hold of the wrong end of the stick' to describe getting something wrong.) Once they had finished with it, the sponge was dipped in a pot of vinegar-water or salt-water for cleaning.

Wet rope

Aboard sailing ships, sailors used a thick, wet rope to wipe themselves. It trailed in salty seawater until needed, and once the job was done, it was dumped back in to get clean.

TOILET PAPER

Toilet paper was first used in China in about the 600s. In Europe, it was first mentioned by the French writer Rabelais in the 1500s (he says it wasn't very good at its job). Toilet paper only became popular about 100 years ago – unsurprisingly, this was about the time the first 'splinter-free' versions were released. Today, it is the most popular form of bottom cleansing. As an alternative, jets, sprays, ladles and other vessels sometimes do the post-poo cleaning.

Clouds of poo

The pygmy sperm whale might be small, but it still has an impressive way to put off predators. It squirts out a big cloud of poo, then fans it around with its tail. The whale hides inside the poo cloud until the predator has, hopefully, gone to look for less-revolting prey.

One diver who got caught in a cloud of whale poo said that:

"The water was like chocolate milk, I couldn't see my hand in front of my face. I had poop in my eyes, mouth, wetsuit: everywhere ..."

Poo beaches

If you ever get to lie on a white, sandy beach on a coral island, just remember: you're lying on a bed of parrotfish poo. As they eat algae from reefs, the parrotfish also bite off tiny bits of coral. These get ground up in their digestive systems, then pooed out and washed ashore as sand.

AH, FRESH AIR!

41

How often do you actually need to poo? The answer depends on what kind of animal you are – and it ranges from 'nearly all the time' to (horrifyingly) 'never'.

All. The. Time.

Some animals are pooing nearly all the time. The ones that poo most are the ones that eat a lot of fibre, such as grass. The fibre passes through their intestines without being digested. Some – cows, for example – hold the food inside for a long time, to get all the nutrients they can from it. Others poo it out quickly so they can gobble it up for a second pass.

Sometimes a lot, sometimes not

Bears, like other mammals, normally poo regularly. However, bears that live in cold areas stay in their dens for part of the year. But bears do not poo in their dens. So during this time, their bottoms plug up with a combination of hair they have swallowed on purpose and dried poo. The bung only comes out months later, when the bear emerges in springtime.

OOOOOH!

Never-ever

Some insects NEVER poo as adults. They live for a short time, reproduce and die. Fortunately the demodex mites that live on your face are among the non-pooing animals.

I MAY FEAST ON YOUR SKIN OILS, BUT AT LEAST I DON'T POO ON YOUR FACE.

GRUESOME POO-SOME: DEADLY CONSTIPATION

Pooing less often than you need is called being constipated. The most extreme (and potentially deadly) form of constipation is Hirschsprung's disease. It affects newborn babies and is caused by an absence of the nerve cells that trigger a poo's passage along the intestines. A traffic-jam of poo builds up, the intestines become puffy and their cells start to die. Hirschsprung's disease is treated using surgery.

How long should it take?

In 2017, researchers found that mammals (including humans) take about 12 seconds to do a complete poo. It doesn't matter how big or small the poo is – from teacup chihuahuas to grizzly bears – pooing took each about 12 seconds. The reason is probably that it's difficult to defend yourself when pooing, so it's best to keep toilet time to a minimum.

IT'S MY TURN! YOU'VE BEEN IN THERE AT LEAST 16 SECONDS!

How much is enough?

For humans, the answer to how MUCH poo you produce each day depends on where you live. In South Asia, a high-fibre diet is common. This bulks up people's poo – and the result is that they apparently produce up to three times as much poo in a day as in certain Western cultures with less fibre-filled diets.

WHAT YOUR POO SAYS ABOUT YOU

Next time you've done your duty, don't flush the poo straight away. You don't want to miss out! Your poo can tell you a lot about you.

In ancient Rome, priests used to 'see the future' in the flight of birds*, thunder and lightning, dreams and odd events. Today, your poo can do a similar job – but it tells you the past, rather than the future.

*NB This does not actually work: just because an eagle flies past, it does not mean you will one day be emperor.

 This imaginary diary of five days of pooing will help you work out what your poo means:

MONDAY

Morning: Nothing.
After lunch: Nothing.
Before bed: Nothing.

If you do not drink enough, your body sucks maximum moisture from your poo, so it moves more slowly. The moisture from the mucus that lines your intestines is sucked back, too, so the dry poo has a less-slippery path.

TUESDAY

Morning: Plip. Plip. Nothing.
After lunch: Ow! Plip, followed by big, painful poo, followed by soft poo.
Before bed: Nothing.

It takes food 24–48 hours to pass through most people. However, if you're constipated, drinking plenty of water can speed things up.

WEDNESDAY, THURSDAY

Morning: Normal poo.
After lunch: Nothing.
Before bed: Nothing.

HAPPY POO = EASY RELEASE

Healthy poo can be smooth or bumpy, but it's comfortably expelled. It contains food waste, water and other stuff (see pages 8–9) in a perfect blend.

FRIDAY

Morning: Nothing.
After lunch: A lot of air and nothing else.
One hour later: Rush to toilet followed by dreadful experience.

SOMETHING YOU ATE? PROBABLY.

Watery poo is called diarrhoea. It often happens suddenly and uncontrollably. Diarrhoea is usually caused by food or drink that upsets the digestive system, or by bad bacteria.

GRUESOME POO-SOME: FLOATERS, NOT SINKERS

What makes a poo float? Two things can lead to a floater: gas or fat.
- Gas is normal and nothing to worry about.
- Fat-based floaters are not normal. Fat causes a stinking, 'oil slick' poo on the water's surface and could mean there is something wrong with your digestive system: if you have this, see a doctor.

THE POO LEXICON

Most humans are reasonably fascinated by poo. In fact, they are so fascinated that there's a whole lexicon of words to describe the different kinds of poo we do. Here are just a few of them:

CLEAN also sometimes called a perfect poo, this comes out so nicely that there is no need to wipe your bottom

DOUBLE-FLUSHER poo so large and/or floaty that one flush will not get rid of it. A sub-type of the double-flusher is the guard dog, a poo that will not go away unless you help it down with a loo brush

FLOATER poo that floats merrily on the surface of the toilet water

GHOST poo that drops like a stone, at the perfect angle to disappear around the bend of the toilet. You can claim the ghost poo was there, but there's no evidence to prove it

HOT sometimes called the chili or curry poo, this one leaves behind a stinging feeling

KRAKATOA poo that explodes out of nowhere, with disastrous results (named after a volcano that erupted unexpectedly in 1883, killing over 35,000 people)

POO OF TERROR also called an Olympic poo, this happens an hour or less before you have to do something nerve-wracking/important

RABBIT DROPPING poo composed of tiny, nut-like nuggets

SECOND COMING poo that seems to have finished ... but then isn't

SHY CHILD poo that you know is up there, but which refuses to come out into the light

SNAKE CHARMER poo that comes out long and stringy, then coils in the toilet like a snoozing snake

SPLASHBACK also sometimes called a bombshell, this is a poo that hits the water like a stone, causing a few drops of water to leap up and sprinkle your bottom

FINDING OUT MORE

More poo facts to read

If you found the information about animal poo in this book fascinating, you might like to get down to the library and borrow a copy of:

The Poo That Animals Do by Paul Mason and Tony De Saulles (Wayland, 2018). It's part of a collection that also includes *The Wee That Animals Pee* and *The Farts that Animals Parp*.

For a random (and sometimes also revolting) collection of information about poo, you could have a look at *It Can't Be True! Poo* by Andrea Mills and Ben Morgan (Dorling Kindersley, 2019). It has some great photos and infographic illustrations.

Poo places to visit

If you ever visit India, you'll find a whole museum dedicated to toilets: Sulabh Bhawan, Palam Dabri Marg, Mahavir Enclave, Palam, New Delhi: 110045

In the UK, there is the Gladstone Pottery Museum, Uttoxeter Road, Longton, Stoke-on-Trent, Staffordshire ST3 1PQ. This is well worth a visit for the 'Flushed with pride' gallery, which lifts the lid on the history of the toilet, although there's plenty more to see here.

Some cities in the UK offer sewer tours – which is not as revolting as you might think. However, the cities that offer these tours change, so to find a tour near you, search for '[name of a nearby city]' + 'sewer tour'.

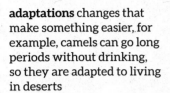

GLOSSARY

adaptations changes that make something easier, for example, camels can go long periods without drinking, so they are adapted to living in deserts

algae a simple plant that usually lives in water; although algae are small, there are sometimes very large numbers of them

astern behind the back end of a ship (the back end is known as the 'stern', the front is the 'bow')

bacteria very small living things, which are made up of just a single cell

biodegradable able to be broken down by nature; plants are biodegradable; for example, if you leave a dead plant outside, it slowly breaks down and becomes part of the soil

blockade in a war, a blockade is a group of ships that aims to stop enemy ships entering or leaving port

briquette a block of squashed-together coal dust that can be burned as fuel

Buddhist a person who follows the religion of Buddhism

by-product something created as a side-effect of a process, for example, eating beans gives you energy, but a by-product of this process is that you fart more

cesspit hole in the ground (usually covered over) in which poo and wee are stored

constipated unable to do a poo

contaminated made dirty or unhealthy

dehydrated lacking water or other liquids

diet name for what kind of food people eat. For example, vegetarians eat a vegetable-based diet

digestive system body system that allows you to get energy and nutrition from food

downstream further down a river, closer to the sea

dung another word for poo, particularly the poo of cows, yaks and similar animals

excrement slightly more polite, scientific word for poo

fertile easily able to grow things

fertiliser something that makes soil more fertile (better at growing plants). Some fertilisers are natural (for example, poo), while others are made in factories

fibre material contained in food that your body cannot digest

fungi group of living things that includes mushrooms, toadstools, mould and yeast

gravity force of attraction that pulls objects towards each other. On Earth, the planet's gravity is stronger than any other

gunpowder explosive material used in bullets and bombs

host living being that provides another with somewhere to live. For example, the shellfish that live on a whale's skin are using the whale as a host

intestine part of your digestive system where nutrients are removed from food and the waste turns into poo

larva(e) second stage in the life cycle of an insect (the stages are egg > larva > pupa > adult insect)

malnourished unhealthy as a result of either not eating enough food or not eating nutritious food

mammal animal with a backbone, hair or fur, and whose young feed on milk from their mother

minuscule very small

nutrient something your body needs in order to grow or to remain healthy

orbit elliptical (an ellipse is like a squashed circle) path around an object

pandemic sudden spread of a dangerous disease across a large area

pressure force of squeezing or squashing

samurai traditional kind of Japanese warrior that existed from the 1300s until 1870

sauropod giant, plant-eating dinosaur

sewer waterway, usually underground, through which wastewater flows

Silk Road trade routes between Europe and Asia, which were used from about 200 BCE until the 1450s

tainted made impure or spoiled in some way

terajoule unit of energy, the same as 1 billion joules (i.e. 1,000,000,000 joules)

toxic poisonous

virus tiny object that can cause disease if it enters a living creature. Scientists have not always agreed about whether viruses are alive or not, but today most think they are not

vomit part-digested food that is expelled from the stomach and through the mouth

wastewater water that has been used by humans, for example when showering, flushing the toilet, washing clothes or at work

whipworm similar animal to a tapeworm (see pages 36–37)

INDEX